gas 1-16-12

"IT'LL BE OKAY."

*How I Kept Obsessive-Compulsive
Disorder (OCD) from Ruining My Life*

Shannon Shy

authorHOUSE®

AuthorHouse™
1663 Liberty Drive, Suite 200
Bloomington, IN 47403
www.authorhouse.com
Phone: 1-800-839-8640

First published by AuthorHouse   3/17/2009

ISBN: 978-1-4389-5731-9 (sc)

Library of Congress Control Number: 2009902266

Printed in the United States of America
Bloomington, Indiana

This book is printed on acid-free paper.

ACKNOWLEDGMENTS

My thanks go out to the following special people: To Debbie, my wife, for her unwavering support throughout my ordeal. To my children, Alex, Andrew, and Samantha, for their patience and support in writing this book. (Also to Andrew—age twelve—for the artwork.) To Debbie (again) and to my good friend Kelly Yasaitis Fanizzo, for their constructive and very-much-needed editorial advice about the organization and content of this book. To the Marines and civilians at the Eastern Area Counsel Office, particularly Rick Hine, Darren Jump, and Craig Jensen, who faithfully supported me in the early stages of my fight against OCD. To my extended family and other lifelong friends from my childhood, high school, college, law school, the Marine Corps, the Navy, the Department of Navy Office of General Counsel, the youth football and baseball communities, and from my neighborhood in Dale City, Virginia (the greatest neighbors in the world)—for the friendship, the great memories, and helping make my life complete. To Joe Galat, President, American Youth Football and Cheerleading, Inc., and Don Hailes, President, Northern

Virginia Youth Athletic Association (my next door neighbor), for the friendship they have given me and the example they have set with their steadfast devotion to the concept of Giving Back. Finally, to the Navy psychiatrists and psychologists and to the civilian psychiatrist who treated me, for their professionalism and wisdom. They helped put me back on path. My eternal gratitude goes to each of them.

DEDICATION

This book is dedicated to my immediate family. To my wife, Debbie, and my children, Alex, Andrew, and Samantha— You give me strength and give my life fulfillment. To my dad and mom, Al and Trudy Shy (may God keep you in eternal peace) and to my sisters, Sheri, Sandy, Sue, and Stacy—Growing up with you gave me a lifetime of wonderful memories and a deep understanding of why "family" is important. Love to you all.

CONTENTS

PREFACE

I have obsessive-compulsive disorder, or OCD as it is commonly known. By 1997, my OCD had progressed to such a severe state that I was on the verge of becoming non-functioning, a non-participant in everyday life. At the time, I was a Major in the U.S. Marine Corps, serving as a lawyer at Camp Lejeune, North Carolina. I had a wife and two young sons. OCD was on the brink of ruining my life (and I was letting it happen). The list of OCD issues affecting me was a mile long. While I discuss those issues in detail in this book, suffice it to say that I could go nowhere and do nothing without finding myself in a seemingly endless loop of intrusive and irrational thoughts, mental anguish, physical pain, and "odd" behaviors.

As a general matter, the anguish, the pain, and the behaviors were caused by OCD convincing me that I bore the responsibility for the "grave" consequences that were sure to result from my failure to take action in response to the intrusive and irrational thoughts. The burdens of the world—especially if it involved the safety of children—became mine. I was on the edge of a total life collapse. I no longer wanted to leave my house, and I no longer wanted human interaction. In fact, at the peak of my OCD affliction, I secretly and repeatedly thought that suicide would be better than the embarrassment, anguish, and pain I was experiencing.

The truth is that I suspected for many years prior to 1997 that I had OCD. Thinking back, I remember experiencing some slight OCD symptoms as early as the mid-1980s, when I was in college. However, I didn't want to admit the possibility that I had OCD (not to myself, not to my wife, not to my friends), and I didn't want any psychiatrist to diagnose me with it. I believed I had too much to lose. I had an outstanding reputation as a Marine officer and lawyer. I had always been a social person and an athlete (high school football player and wrestler and collegiate wrestler), and I was considered a leader throughout my academic years (president of my high school class my freshman and sophomore years and president of the student council my senior year, a captain on my high school football and wrestling teams, Missouri Boy's State Representative, and president of the Student Bar Association in law school). Most importantly, I had a family to support—a wife and two young sons.

Although I couldn't understand what was happening to me and even though I was embarrassed by my "odd" behavior, I had convinced myself that *being diagnosed* with some sort of mental disorder would not only cause me to lose my career and destroy my family, but also would be shameful. I believed the Navy medical community (the Navy provides medical services for

Marines) would find me "unfit for duty" and I would be viewed by the world to be incapable, weak, and a catastrophic failure.

I was frustrated and confused beyond compare. *How could this happen? I wasn't weak! How could I have a mental disorder that transformed me from the "regular" outgoing guy that I had been into a man with inexplicable irrational thoughts and quirky behaviors that dominated nearly every moment of my life? I would be letting everyone down—my family, fellow Marines, childhood friends, college and law school friends, etc.—if it became known that I had something mentally wrong with me. Surely I would be a resounding disappointment.* These thoughts prevented me from seeking help.

Finally, in 1997, after some polite nudging from my wife and a colleague (neither of whom had mentioned anything about my behaviors to the other), after recognizing that I was becoming a non-functioning person paralyzed by life itself, and after one very memorable OCD episode, I sought help and confronted my OCD. Although I believed it would be the end of my career, I called a psychiatrist. I was put on medication and began behavioral therapy. In a short period of time, absorbing the advice I had received and through trial and error, I developed and implemented a successful strategy to cope with and manage the OCD that tried to ruin my life. I call my strategy "Ground Rules and Checkpoints." With the help of my doctors, with the support of my friends and family, and with my strategy, I turned my life around 180 degrees.

I say with 100 percent certainty that I never would have achieved all that I did after 1997 had I not sought help and taken a stand against OCD. This book tells the story of how I dealt with and ultimately came to successfully manage my OCD. I had thought about writing a book about my experiences just a few years after I figured out how to manage my OCD. I opted not to, however, because I didn't think the book would have the credibility it needed if I couldn't show that the strategy had any sustaining power. It's been more than a decade now that I've used my strategy, and approximately six years that I have been absolutely medication free.

Being diagnosed with OCD didn't cause me to lose anything. I didn't disappoint the world, and I wasn't seen as a catastrophic failure. Being diagnosed with OCD didn't cause me to be belittled or ridiculed or to feel ashamed. And most importantly, I didn't let OCD ruin my life. By May 1998, when I transferred from Camp Lejeune to the Pentagon, my Ground Rules and Checkpoints were helping me effectively battle OCD. After September 1999, I was seeing a psychiatrist, but basically only to get medication refills. During the early 2000s, I worked with my doctor to reduce my medication levels. I weaned myself off medication to the point that I barely took it. Finally, by early 2003, I was absolutely medication free and finally stopped seeing a doctor.

I have lived a very happy, successful, and productive life for many years and continue to do so. OCD no longer adversely affects my life. My strategy to combat OCD worked, and it continues to work. How can I say that? With the utmost humility, I can say the following:

➤ In 1999, my wife and I decided to settle our family down in Dale City, Virginia, about twenty-five miles south of Washington, DC after I applied for and was offered a great job as a civilian attorney with the Department of the Navy. I resigned my active-duty commission and then accepted a Marine Corps Reserve commission.

➤ In 2000, I was the *only* officer out of more than three hundred eligible Marine Corps Reserve Majors to be "deep selected" (from beneath the promotion zone) for promotion to Lieutenant Colonel. In addition to my normal reserve duties at the Pentagon, I became a "utility infielder" for the Marine Corps and filled gaps in various leadership positions. I served as Acting Counsel for the Pacific Area Counsel Office in Okinawa in 2003, Acting Deputy Counsel for the Commandant of the Marine Corps in 2004, and Acting Officer-in-Charge of a mobilization detachment in 2006 and 2007. In 2007, I retired as a Reserve Lieutenant Colonel with twenty-one years of service and was awarded the Legion of Merit Medal upon my retirement.

➤ My career as a civilian attorney took off and has been extremely successful and fulfilling. I have had the privilege of serving in senior positions with tremendous amounts of responsibility and in fast-paced, stressful environments. I served as an occupational safety and health attorney for five years at the Naval Sea Systems Command in Washington, DC (the command overseeing all of the naval shipyards, surface warfare centers, and undersea warfare centers, among other things). I then moved over to the Pentagon for nearly three years to serve as the U.S. Marine Corps' senior land use and environmental attorney in the Office of Counsel for the Commandant responsible for all such legal issues affecting Marine Corps interests worldwide. I am now back at the Naval Sea Systems Command, serving in a supervisory capacity as the command's senior environmental and occupational safety and health attorney.

➤ I became very involved in working with the children of our community. In addition to serving as the leader of a Cub Scout pack, I coached youth football, baseball, and soccer teams. In 2002, I was the head coach of a youth football team that won a Virginia state championship. In 2003, I co-founded a non-profit youth football organization that now manages eight football teams with over two hundred children, that won four national championships between 2005 and 2007 and also focuses on excellence in academics, and community service (with special thanks to our coaches, kids, and parents). I have helped organize some wonderful local, national, and international projects that include a football field refurbishment project, a clothing drive for Hurricane Katrina victims, and a toy drive for Sri Lankan children orphaned by the 2004 tsunami.

➤ From 2007 to 2009, I served as National Membership Director for American Youth Football, Inc. (AYF), a youth organization with more than 515,000 participants worldwide. I worked with folks in different parts of the United States and in other countries who were trying to start football and cheer programs. I also have had and will continue to have the great privilege of helping run the weeklong AYF national championships each year. Finally, as a hobby, I serve as a stadium announcer for the local high school football games and the AYF national championships and AYF national all-star game.

➤ And while the above are significant parts of my living a productive life, they don't compare to the most important benefit of my successful management of OCD. Most important for me is that OCD no longer stands as an obstacle to me being the husband and dad that I can and should be. My relationship with my wife Debbie has never been stronger. We will celebrate our twenty-year anniversary in 2009. In 2005, we added a daughter to our brood. I have a terrific and close relationship with each of our three athletic, brilliant, and well-adjusted kids: Alex, sixteen; Andrew, twelve; and Samantha, three.

Why I Wrote this Book

I am a "people person." I find it extremely rewarding and gratifying to help others in need—family, friends, and strangers— be it a helping hand, an ear to listen, or a word of encouragement. In this spirit, I have shared my story with a few others who suffer from this debilitating disorder. These individuals told me that my words and the approach I offered helped them find a new path forward. One person told me I changed her life. I have also had the opportunity to share my story and approach with the parent of a teenager with OCD. That parent told me that my words were extremely helpful to her in both *understanding* her daughter's ordeal and *assisting* her daughter through it. The positive responses I have received from these people prompted me to finally write the book. It is my sincere hope that someone suffering from OCD, particularly someone who believes his or her life may also be on the brink of ruin, or a person close to someone with OCD, will learn from and be helped by my experience. In my view, if one person finds this book helpful, it will have been worth writing.

Please note that this book is *not* intended as psychiatric advice or any other type of medical advice. While I describe in basic terms what was explained to me by the professionals with whom I consulted, this book is not intended to be a medical source about the causes of OCD, the treatment of OCD, or medications available to treat OCD. I strongly recommend that anyone who believes he or she might be suffering from OCD seek professional help. I have great respect for the fields of psychiatry and psychology, for they got me on the road to recovery.

This book *is* intended to provide *hope, comfort, confidence, insight, and information about some practical tools that were useful to me* for those who suffer from the ruthless enemy we call OCD and for those who are trying to help someone who suffers from OCD. This is a good-news story with many lessons and a terrific ending! For those who have OCD, this story lets you know that having OCD doesn't mean you are crazy. Having OCD doesn't mean that your life or career is over. It doesn't mean you are weak, unfit, or incapable. This story lets you know that you don't need to feel embarrassed about having OCD. (There are millions of people just like you.) You too can have the courage to confront OCD and tell yourself that "IT'S OKAY" if those horrible, intrusive, and irrational thoughts come into your mind. They are not your thoughts. They are OCD's thoughts. This book lets you know that "IT'LL BE OKAY" when you resist the compulsion to act in response to those thoughts. Most importantly, it is a story that lets you know that you too can keep OCD from ruining your life. For those of you who are helping someone who has OCD, this story lets you know that you *can* help the person you love.

CHAPTER 1

AS YOU BEGIN YOUR JOURNEY
Avoiding Some Pitfalls

Before I get into the details of my OCD—symptoms, treatment, and strategy—I want to alert you to some pitfalls I encountered when I started reading about OCD shortly after my diagnosis but before I began treatment. These "pitfalls" both demoralized and devastated me and caused me to spiral downward to a place I refer to as the "bottom of the bottom." The downward spiral occurred because I did not have enough information to properly deal with what I had read.

Pitfall #1—*The Power of Suggestion*. The power of suggestion can strongly come into play with OCD. Shortly after I was diagnosed, I went to a bookstore and read about the OCD symptoms of others, including some utterly despicable thoughts. Reading about these thoughts not only alarmed me, it also caused me to immediately think "Oh God, I can't have that thought." The problem arises when one tries to resist an OCD thought once it is in one's head or tries to avoid having the thought in the first place. In my case, this was a futile effort. If I tried to resist the thought or tried to avoid having a thought, it most assuredly meant that I would have the thought. The point here is this: do not fret if OCD takes advantage of the *power of suggestion and introduces thoughts to you that you had never experienced before.* If you have an OCD thought as a result of reading about the symptoms of others, *it's okay.* Identify the horrible thought as an OCD thought and allow the thought to be in your mind. Do not resist it. It doesn't mean it is your thought and it doesn't mean you agree with it. As you'll learn in this book, identifying the thought as an OCD thought and allowing the thought to be in my mind are two key steps in my management of OCD.

Pitfall #2—*Cure.* Do not get wrapped around the word *cure. Cure* is a relative term, and it depends on how you want to define it. In my view, the term *cure* is only meaningful in the OCD context if you measure the term by the degree to which you successfully manage OCD and ultimately the degree to which it affects your life. *OCD can be managed successfully such that one can live virtually symptom-free and managed in a way that OCD absolutely does not affect your life.* To me, that is a "cure."

What tripped me up initially was that the very first book I perused at the bookstore stated that OCD cannot be cured. I was demoralized. *I'm going to be like this forever?!* Thank goodness the answer to that question was and is "no." And I didn't need to be demoralized (and you don't need to be demoralized either) because the issue of "cure" must be considered in the proper context. The medical profession has not yet, with absolute certainty, put its finger on the cause of OCD. While OCD generally is treated with medication and behavioral therapy, there is no drug, herb, or magical incantation (in other words, a "cure") that makes OCD go away forever. Again, the real key is whether one can learn to successfully manage OCD symptoms and ultimately lead a life virtually free of OCD symptoms, to the point that OCD does not affect one's quality of life. I have learned to do so (without medication since 2003) and, again, that is a "cure" to me.

CHAPTER 2

MY SYMPTOMS

"OCD? So, what, did you wash your hands a lot?"

When I tell people today that I struggled with OCD, I usually get asked about my symptoms. More times than not, folks specifically mention a very common OCD symptom and ask, "OCD? So, what, did you wash your hands a lot?" This chapter describes my OCD symptoms and the next chapter describes the OCD episode that finally caused me to decide to seek help. These two chapters explicitly describe how OCD tortured me. I discuss these symptoms in detail because in order to understand how significant my turnaround was, one must understand how deeply and darkly I was affected by OCD. If you are trying to help someone you believe may have OCD, the detailed descriptions will give you an idea about how OCD works. Having OCD was exhausting. The intrusive, irrational thoughts were haunting and caused embarrassment, anguish, and physical pain. Physically, my heart rate increased, my heart pounded as if my chest was going to burst open, my body temperature rose, I perspired, and my stomach tied itself into knots. (For those of you with OCD, remember, as I discuss my symptoms, it's okay if the power of suggestion puts some or all of these thoughts in your head. Allow them to be there. *It doesn't mean you agree with those thoughts.* They are not *your* thoughts.)

1.   ***Objects on the Side of the Road.*** *Every* time I would drive, I would see something on the side of the road, which I would immediately identify as the object it was (a log, for example) and then a thought would come to me that it might be a person laying there dying or dead. I would turn the car around again and again and again (twenty to thirty times would not be a stretch) to go back and look at it, to confirm that it was not a dead or dying person.

2.   ***Hitting Bumps in the Road While Driving My Car.*** *Every* time I ran over a noticeable bump while driving my car, I would think immediately that I might have hit a person. My first reaction would be to look in the rearview mirror to ensure I didn't hit anyone. That, of course, would be followed by a line of reasoning that would convince me that I had a bad view in the mirror and therefore would have to turn around to go check— again and again and again. When I would arrive at my destination, the first thing I would do is get out of the car and check to ensure there wasn't a body part, blood, or a piece of clothing on the bumper. I then waited for hours, sometimes days, sure that the police would arrive at my door and arrest me for hit and run.

3.   ***Bodies of Water.*** Pools, ponds, lakes, rivers, and oceans caused me great grief. *Every* time I would drive by or be near a

body of water, I would see something that caused me to think that a person was in distress. Again, if I was in my car, I would turn around to go back for another look, repeatedly, until I was able to convince myself on a prayer that a person was not drowning. Sometimes I would drive by a body of water and deliberately not look into the water (thinking that if I didn't look, I couldn't see anything that might be a problem). That didn't work. I would merely think that my failure to look was a deliberate act that prevented me from seeing the person in distress, so therefore, I was more culpable in the distressed person's death.

4. ***Accountability of People Swimming.*** Related to issue number three, I could not go to a pool, a lake, or an ocean without keeping careful watch of who went into the water and who came out of the water. I remember being at the beach along the Atlantic Ocean at Camp Lejeune and losing track of two women who I had seen go in the water. I approached the lifeguard, and said, "It's probably nothing, but I saw two women go in the water about a half hour ago. I never saw them come out." He gave me a long blank stare. "Are you telling me that you think two women drowned out there?" he asked. "No," I replied. "I just wanted you to know what I saw." "Thanks," he said, with a hint of sarcasm in his voice. "We'll keep an eye out." He looked at the other lifeguard as if to say, "What a nut." I walked away embarrassed, but at least I was relieved to know that I let someone know about the two women. I told myself that their lives were no longer *my responsibility.*

5.   ***Risk of Fire.*** The risk of fire commanded my attention in all venues—at work, at home, in businesses, at gas stations, and while traveling down the road (particularly in wildfire-crazy California, where I was stationed from 1992 to 1994 and visited quite often on business afterward). If I saw anything that had the potential of sparking or catching fire, no matter how remote that possibility might have been—coffeepots, irons, stoves and ovens, discarded cigarettes and matches, candles, electrical cords, and overused outlets—I focused on it. If I saw it, I wouldn't rest until I brought it to someone's attention.

I remember once leaving a business, going home, and then finally succumbing to the thoughts, the anguish, and the pain, driving about ten miles back to the business to let them know that they might want to check the plugs in a particular outlet that wasn't in plain view. In classic OCD form, there were days I could not even get to my car in the driveway without going back inside the house numerous times to make sure the coffeepot, the stove, and the iron were off. There were even times when I would get halfway to my office, only to have my OCD tell me that the coffeepot or stove might be on, and as a consequence, my house would burn down and my family would be in grave danger. In response to this, I would either call my wife or turn around myself to go home to check it.

Gas stations were always an OCD-rich experience for me. If I dripped any gasoline (even a drop) while returning the gas nozzle to the pump, I would report it to the attendant. After returning the nozzle to the pump and putting the gas cap back on my tank, I would check and re-check several times to make sure both were in place before I would get into my car. Also, I would avoid driving over the covers to the underground gasoline storage tanks out of fear that I would dislodge the cover, causing either gas vapors to leak out or someone to step on the cover and fall in. If I did by chance happen to drive over a cover, I would go into the gas station and tell the attendant what I had just done. To make matters worse, gas presented a dual threat for me. Gas either meant there was a risk of fire or explosion or it meant there was an environmental/safety hazard, which leads me to my next group of symptoms.

6.   *Environmental/Safety Hazards.* Anything that looked like it could cause an environmental or safety concern became, for all intents and purposes, my sole focus. For example, a discarded container of any chemical, such as antifreeze, on the side of the road, broken glass, spills of any liquid on a floor or walkway, missing gas caps, gas spilled on the ground (even just a few drops and even at a gas station), and the smell of gasoline (even at a gas station) received my undivided attention. Basically, I was in physical pain, sweating, and in great distress until I brought the issue to the attention of someone who had responsibility for the area. Here are a few anecdotes to give you a clearer image of my condition.

    o   In 1995, I was getting ready to mow the lawn of the house I was renting. I filled the lawnmower's gas tank, started the engine, and proceeded to mow, only to discover quickly that I forgot to put the gas cap back on the tank. A small amount of gas (less than an ounce) splashed on the ground. Within seconds, I concluded that the gas would seep through the ground into the ground water and poison the entire community. I had moved the mower about two feet, so it wasn't as if I could point to one particular small spot on the ground to identify where the gas was. I knelt down with my nose nearly touching the earth and proceeded to smell the ground to see where the gas had spilled. I then dug a hole with a perimeter about one foot outside where I figured the gas had spilled and about one foot deep. I put the partially contaminated dirt in a trash bag (lined by another trash bag) and took it to the dump to turn it in as hazardous waste. After I got back home, and for the next week, I conducted my sniff tests to make sure I had removed all of the gas. Seven months later, I conducted the sniff test on this spot once again prior to moving out of the house.

o   I was an environmental lawyer for the Marine Corps at Camp Lejeune. As Marines do, we would go out for a three- to five-mile run around noon every day. I dreaded going. First, we usually ran near the water (we've already discussed this problem). Second, I could not go for a run without inspecting every piece of trash that was lying on the ground, to make sure it wasn't something that could cause an environmental spill. One of the Majors in my office used to rib me (in a good-natured way), saying, "Shannon is the Camp Lejeune trash man" and "Shannon never saw a piece of trash he didn't like."

o   On one occasion, I noticed some broken glass laying

sporadically over a half-mile stretch of a dirt path used by joggers and cyclists at Camp Lejeune. The thought that a Marine or civilian family member or base employee might fall and cut themselves or blow out a bicycle tire plagued me all day until late in the evening. From my home, I telephoned the Base Officer of the Day and reported it. "Okaaaayyy," he said, not knowing what to make of my report. "I'll let Base Safety know about it and I'm sure they'll send someone there to clean up the glass on Monday." I was embarrassed, *but at least the blood of the soon-to-be injured was off of my hands.*

o   In 1996, my younger sister and her family visited us in Jacksonville, North Carolina. I was giving them a windshield tour of the base when I saw what looked like a bag of lawn fertilizer lying on the side of the road, across from one of the ammunition supply points. I turned the car around, stopped, got out, and sure enough, it was a half-empty bag of fertilizer. I immediately thought about the fact that fertilizer was one of the ingredients to make the explosives used in the 1994 Oklahoma City bombings. Over the course of an hour, as we continued to sightsee and then drove toward my house, I struggled, openly and verbally, in the presence of my sister and her husband as to whether I should report this to the military police. It was all they could do to keep me from calling. My sister, noticing this peculiar behavior that she had not witnessed before in me, asked, "Is everything okay with you?" I did not call and for the next several *weeks,* I simply awaited the report that the ammunition supply point had been hit by a terrorist and then about how much I would be shamed because I could have prevented it.

    o   I helped coach my five-year-old son's soccer team. While the head coach warmed up the team prior to each game, I would walk every square inch of the soccer field to ensure that there were no rocks or other objects that could hurt the kids. If I ran out of time and was unable to check a particular part of the field, I would tell the head coach and referee that I had found some rocks on one part of the field but was unable to check the other part. I hated the looks they would give me, but at least *it would not be my fault if one of the kids fell and got hurt.*

7.   ***Safety Issues with Other Vehicles.*** I constantly kept a watchful eye out for problems with other vehicles. Missing gas caps, objects hanging low or dragging beneath or behind the vehicle, and tire abnormalities were just a few of the problems that garnered my attention. I remember getting behind a newer pickup truck on the way home from work in Jacksonville one evening. It appeared as if the left back tire on the truck was wobbling. I tried to wave at the driver but to no avail. I followed him off the route that I would normally take, down a few country roads, and finally into a not-so-well-lit industrial park. He jumped out of the truck and ran back to my car. "What the f*** do you want?" he demanded, ready to fight. "You've been following me for thirty minutes." Rather embarrassed, I simply said, "I was trying to get your attention. Your left rear tire looks like it was wobbling." He glanced at his tire, which had some dirt on it (thus causing the optical illusion of a wobble as the tire rolled) and said, "My

tire is fine. Mind your own f***in' business! You're going to get yourself killed following people like this." My wife agreed with this assessment after I told her this story when I *finally* got home that night.

8.   ***Checking Cars Parked on the Roadside.*** Cars parked on the side of the road presented huge dilemmas for me. Some roadside cars have occupants; some do not. Some are broken down; some are simply sitting there while the driver waits for someone. For me, *every* car on the side of the road was a potential site of a person who might be dead or dying. If there was a car stopped on the side of the road, it received a quick glance from me to see if anyone was inside (possibly in need of help). More times than I care to remember, I would rightly conclude that the car was empty, but then be convinced that I either didn't get a good look or maybe that I did see a person. This, of course, led to countless checks and re-checks, only to discover the car was empty, or more often than not, that the "person" I saw was just a headrest on the seat. The distant sight of a car on the roadside used to make my stomach turn because I knew what awaited me.

I remember once seeing a car on the side of the road in Jacksonville. A man (yes, I actually did know this was a person) was lying back in the driver's seat with his head tilted back. I drove on. Quickly convinced that the man was probably dead, I decided to go back and check. I turned around, drove back, stopped my car, approached the driver's side window, and tapped on the door. The guy sprang up and nearly came through the open window at me. "What are you doing?" he screamed. Stuttering through it, I said, "I thought you were hurt." "Well, I'm not. I'm sleeping. Leave me be," he replied. This story also prompted my wife to tell me that "Someday, someone is going to shoot you."

9.   ***Kids and Animals Left in Cars.*** I dreaded driving or walking through parking lots because of my focus on the possibility that there might be kids or animals left in cars. I would avoid going to grocery stores, malls, and other businesses because of this reason alone. I could not walk through a parking lot, particularly during the summer, without *going out of my way* to look in car windows or listen carefully for sounds of distress, to ensure there were no kids or animals left in cars. If I wasn't convinced that I did a good enough job of looking or listening after going into the store or getting back into my car to leave, I would return to the parking lot to try to satisfy my doubt.

10.   ***How Parents Treat Their Kids.*** This will sound odd coming from a father who at the time had two small children, but I dreaded going to places where there were children. I knew that I would become focused (to the exclusion of my own family and even to the exclusion of why I was there in the first place) on the actions or words of other parents in dealing with their kids. I would actively watch and listen to how parents were interacting with their children. I *always* found a reason to be concerned. It got to the point where I would try not to focus on what others were saying around me so I wouldn't hear anything objectionable, which resulted in me *only* focusing on what others were saying.

One incident stands out in my mind. I still regret the way I handled it, because my behavior affected one of my sons.

When my oldest son was four, he got really sick. I took him to the emergency room at the naval hospital on Camp Lejeune. While we were in the waiting room, a woman across the room behind me was trying to deal with her rambunctious small children. I listened to her repeatedly tell the kids to settle down, and then at one point I thought I heard her say (or my OCD convinced me that she said) something about slapping her child in the face. *Did she really say that?* I glanced in the direction of where the comment was made. I was alarmed by what I thought I had heard, but I didn't do or say anything about it initially.

Over the next ten to fifteen minutes (at which point my son's name was called to be seen) I struggled over whether to do anything about the mother. I became convinced that my inaction would result in those children being beaten and tortured by their mother. I told my son's nurse what I thought I may have heard, although I did not know where the mother had gone. She agreed that the woman should not have said what she said (if she even said it), but indicated if I didn't have a name or couldn't point the woman out, there was nothing they could do. I immediately panicked, thinking that my failure to act back in the waiting room meant that those children were in danger of being beaten for the rest of their childhood. (And it would be my fault and when people found out that I could have done something to stop it, I would be shamed out of the Marine Corps.) I told the nurse that I would be right back. I left my son on the gurney in the ER with her so that I could go find the woman and then point her out to the hospital staff.

After searching for a while, I found her on another floor of the hospital. I confronted her and her husband. She denied ever saying it and her husband told me that such accusations were pretty serious and he did not understand why I would make something like that up. Embarrassed, I left them and returned to my son. I had been gone about fifteen minutes. He was crying because I had left him for such a long time, and the nurse was fuming. I felt two inches tall.

11. **_Locked Doors._** Whether it was leaving home or leaving work, I checked, rechecked, and checked some more to make sure doors were locked. I would almost instantaneously play out the potential consequences (e.g., murderer entering the house and mutilating my family) of leaving a door unlocked. Again it would not be a stretch to say that I rechecked door locks up to twenty to thirty times before I would finally move on, still unsure whether the door was locked. I often would twist the knob and violently push and pull on the knob while saying aloud to myself, "I'm holding the knob and pushing the door. It is locked. It is locked." I would get into my car, begin to drive off, and I would think, *You were concentrating so hard on the words you were saying, you didn't pay attention to whether the door was actually locked.* I would turn around and go check it again. This became life-altering in 1993 and 1994 in California after my first son started walking and we

lived just off of a well-traveled road. It once took me about forty-five minutes to actually get further than a quarter mile away from my house, because I turned around so many times to check the door.

12.   ***Perceived Defects in the Wings of Airplanes.*** I traveled frequently for the Marine Corps. *Every* time I got on a plane, I would visually inspect the wing while sitting in my seat to ensure there were no defects such as cracks. I remember at least two occasions where, after OCD convinced me that the plane crash was going to be my fault if I didn't disclose what I had discovered, I called the flight attendant (once pre-flight and once in-flight) to point out what appeared to be a crack in the wing. On both occasions, the flight attendants explained that the plane underwent a thorough pre-flight safety inspection and it would be "okay."

13.   ***Proofreading Documents.*** As an attorney, I wrote many legal opinions, some rather lengthy. That wasn't problematic, because conscientious attorneys write thorough legal opinions. What was problematic was when I would make one or two changes in a document. Instead of simply printing the page with the change, I would print the entire document and then read every word of the document each time it was printed. I was convinced there was a potential that making the change(s) might cause the document to change in some other way and that this would result in providing incorrect legal advice (which, in turn, might result in the client taking a course of action that either got the client in trouble or would result in environmental harm). I was convinced

that if I didn't print and read the entire document word for word (again), I would not know with certainty whether there had been any other deletions or changes. It would take me hours upon hours to get a document finalized.

14.   ***Contamination/Poison.*** I can't count how many times a day I washed my hands, out of fear that I would contaminate or poison other people, especially my children. If I came into contact with any anything remotely related to waste, dirt, bacteria, or a chemical substance (including animals, fish, reptiles, and even containers holding the waste, dirt, bacteria, or chemical), I would go to great lengths to remove all traces of the source. I washed my hands when most folks do (when they are actually dirty, such as after using the restroom) and when most folks don't. It became ritualistic. I would wash my hands and then wipe down any surface that I might have contacted, such as doorknobs, countertops, spray bottles that held the chemical, the sink, the faucet handles, and the soap dispenser. I would then wash my hands again to complete the cycle.

The concern over contamination and poison wasn't just limited to my hands. It extended to my clothes and shoes. If my clothes or shoes came into contact with anything "dirty," I would change them as soon as possible (and clean anything with which they came into contact.) When walking on or across a parking lot, driveway, or road, I was extremely careful not to step in or let my children step in any type of fluid leakage or spill on the ground or even a slight stain from a previous leak or spill. If I did, I would immediately take my shoes off, and as soon as I got

home, either clean them with soap and water (which, in turn, triggered issues about releasing contaminants into the sewage system, or if I used a hose in the yard, about contaminating the earth and ground water). If I didn't feel like worrying about the issues related to washing my shoes, I would simply throw the shoes away. (Yet another reason to avoid my garage, gas stations, and parking lots.)

15. ***Checking Out of Hotels or Rented Houses.*** As I already stated, I traveled quite often with the Marine Corps. Consequently, I stayed in countless hotel rooms. As an additional by-product of serving in the military, my family moved a lot. We lived in six different rented houses between 1989 and 1997. Interestingly, notwithstanding issue number fourteen above, I was never concerned about whether the rooms or houses had any existing contamination when I got there. What sent me into the "endless loop" was trying to check out of the room or the house, recognizing that I would never return. The finality of leaving the place and the thought that I might have left the room or house in an unsafe (e.g., forgetting to turn off an iron, coffeepot, lamp, or the stove, or forgetting to lock the doors and windows), unsanitary (e.g., forgetting to flush the toilet or spilling something and the carpet getting moldy), or damaged (even just a nick) condition caused me to revisit and re-inspect the room or the house over and over and over.

In 1995, when my wife and I moved from Charlottesville, Virginia to Jacksonville, North Carolina (after living in a rented house for only nine months), it took me four days to get the house in "perfect" condition and nearly a half a day to stop going back into the house to re-inspect everything. I made the same circuit through the house each time, checking every light in every room, checking the stove, checking the water, checking the windows, and checking the locks. Oh, and yes, as I mentioned before, I even conducted another "sniff" test on the lawn because it was here where I had spilled a small amount of gasoline seven months before.

16. ***Standing "Duty" as the Command Officer-of-the-Day.*** Standing "duty" is a regular part of life in the military. It requires one to report to the command headquarters building once a month or so to serve as the Commanding Officer's after-hours representative from the close of business until the morning of the following day. A normal tour of duty generally encompasses presiding over evening/morning Colors, windshield inspections of the geographic area of responsibility for the command, answering phones, handling Red Cross notifications and emergency travel, etc. The officer of the day records significant events in a duty logbook, which is turned in to the command Chief of Staff or Executive Officer at the end of the duty period. For most officers, an average logbook for a tour of duty would run one to two pages.

Enter my OCD. I dreaded standing duty. The average length of my logbook entries ran somewhere around seven pages. For me, practically every phone call, observation, and occurrence was at least potentially significant and worth verifying, re-verifying, or otherwise worth reporting. It got to the point—so I was told by a

Gunnery Sergeant who stood duty with me a few times at Camp Pendleton in 1993 and 1994—where staff noncommissioned officers would check the duty roster to see if they had duty with me. If they did, they would do everything within their power to switch dates.

I remember a particular incident in 1995 while standing duty at the Army's Judge Advocate General School in Charlottesville, Virginia (I was attending the school working on a Master of Laws degree in 1994–95). On one of my rounds inside the building in the middle of the night, I looked out a window into the parking lot and saw someone placing a large brown paper grocery bag into a dumpster. Initially, I thought it was probably a resident student throwing away some trash. My OCD tried to convince me that someone may have been placing a bomb in the dumpster. After an hour of fretting that I had witnessed the next Oklahoma City bombing in progress and failed to do anything about it, I finally went out and climbed into the dirty dumpster only to find out that the "bomb" was really just a bag of trash.

CHAPTER 3

THE EPISODE THAT TRIGGERED
MY DECISION TO SEEK HELP

Someone's Bleeding to Death

October 23, 1997, Jacksonville, North Carolina. (Told in the first person present so you can stand in my shoes and experience this as I did.)

I am a Major in the U.S. Marine Corps. I've been on active duty for almost nine years and a Major for a little more than a year. My oldest son is five years old and my youngest son recently turned one. It's 5:45 AM, still dark, on a cool October morning in Jacksonville, North Carolina. I want to get to my office on Camp Lejeune by 6:00 AM to put the final touches on a memo due to one of my senior clients by 8:00 AM.

I dread going out of the house because I know *something* is going to happen. It is an eleven-mile drive to my office. I get into my car and begin the painful trek. *What's it going to be today? A dead body on the side of the road? Someone drowning in the New River? A wheel about to fall off a car? A strong smell of gasoline fumes in the air? Just get to work.* My stomach is already in knots.

I get about three miles from the industrial park toward the direction of Camp Lejeune and see a pay phone at a gas station parking lot. *Police? 9-1-1? They're going to laugh at me. The only thing I have to report is a noise that sounded like lumber. I can't call 9-1-1.* I look in the phone book for the non-emergency number for the police department and dial the phone. It rings and rings and rings. No answer. I'm relieved because I at least attempted to call the police and now I don't have to be embarrassed about reporting the "mystery of the falling lumber." I get back in my car and continue toward work. It's 6:15 AM. *Damn it! I'm late.*

As I drive toward the base, my heart is pounding so hard it feels like it is going to burst out of my chest. Like every other time I discover a problem and fail to do something about it, I get hot flashes, my chest tightens, I start to sweat, and I have a knot in my stomach. *There is still someone dying back there and the murderer is loose—probably breaking into someone's house getting ready to kill again. In fact, he's probably killing someone else right now. You have to go back and help the person dying in the industrial park or at least report it.* "F***, f***, f***!" I scream, pounding my fist on the dashboard. "What's wrong with me?!" I turn the car around and head back to the industrial park. In a strip mall parking lot near the industrial park I see two patrol cars with their parking lights on. I take a deep breath, pull into the lot, and prepare to embarrass myself. *I can hear the officers now, "You heard a gunshot and saw a suspect almost an hour ago, and now* *you're reporting it? What's wrong with you? And you're a Marine? You better hope that person is not dead."*

It is now past 6:30 AM. I approach the officers and attempt to determine how best to convey the information in a way that will prompt them to check it out, but not alarm them and not emphasize my own dereliction. "May I help you?" one officer asks. I begin the way I've begun when alerting someone in authority about a self-imposed "problem" so many times before … "It's probably nothing, but I just wanted to let you know what I heard and what I saw about forty-five minutes ago …" I explain about the noise that sounded like a piece of lumber but that could have been a gunshot, and about the guy I saw walking. The officers look at each other and the driver turns to me and says, "I'm sure it's okay. We would have heard something about it if it was a gunshot." I thank them, walking away embarrassed but relieved. *I let them know about it; if they don't want to do anything about it, that's on them.*

The hot flashes and the pounding heart go away. *Until the next thing happens, that is.* I feel as though I have a tortured soul. For the first time in thirteen years, since my mother's early death, tears begin to well up in my eyes. As I completed my drive to my office on that morning in October 1997, I finally concluded that I needed professional help. *Your career is over. You are such a failure as a father and husband. What a disappointment.* But I concluded I had no other reasonable choices. I had boiled it down to either being seen by a doctor, living forever in my own prison of anguish and pain, or simply ending it all. Later that morning, from my office, I called the psychiatric unit at the Camp Lejeune Naval Hospital. It was the smartest decision I ever made.

CHAPTER 4

THE PHONE CALL AND
FIRST DOCTOR'S VISIT

"I Don't Trust Psychiatrists"

That morning I spoke by phone with a Navy psychiatrist (an active-duty Lieutenant) at the naval hospital. I told him that I was having some "issues" and I needed to talk to someone. I began by telling him that I did not trust psychiatrists. I said that I believed they were too quick to diagnose problems as mental illnesses and did so in order to validate their own profession. (I really had nothing to base that on, but fear was driving me to self-preservation.) In a rather direct, stern tone of voice, I told him that if I came to talk to him, he had better be sure of his diagnosis, because I did not want to lose my career over a hasty diagnosis. Calmly and reassuringly, he indicated that he simply wanted to talk to me, and we scheduled an appointment for the following day.

When I went to see the psychiatrist, I was certain that he would label me with some disorder. I truly believed it would be the end of my career. I was confident I would be told to leave the Marine Corps and no one would ever hire me as a civilian attorney (or for any other job, for that matter). This, I was sure, would lead to my inability to support my family and ultimately lead to my divorce and my children being taken away from me. Yet, given the options I had settled upon and believed I was facing, I felt I had to take my chances with the psychiatrist. Fortunately, it turned out not to be a "roll of the dice." It was a safe, wise, and prudent decision.

I began the session repeating my distrust of psychiatry and warning him that if he was going to diagnose me with a mental illness, he'd better be sure he's right. I told him that I was concerned that a diagnosis of mental illness would end my career, make me unemployable, and destroy my family. To say I tried to emphasize these points would be an understatement. I told the doctor that I had prepared a list of the odd thoughts and behaviors that were controlling my life and which I thought might be problematic. He said he didn't need to see the list. He simply wanted me to talk to him. This gave me great concern, because I didn't think he would be able to diagnose me correctly without the list.

I told him what I thought was important about my situation. First, I described in painstaking detail (to compensate for him declining to take my list) the outrageous thoughts and "odd" behaviors I had been experiencing. Second, I explained that within seconds (literally) of seeing or hearing something that concerned me, my mind would extrapolate consequences out multiple tiers to the eventual worst-case scenario. It was almost as if it each concern was a complex math equation and my brain was a computer programmed only for doom and gloom. Finally, I used an analogy of a photograph and the photograph's negative to compare how "normal" people perceived their everyday surroundings with the way I perceived my surroundings. Assume that the distortions and highlights present in the photograph's negative represented potential problems that might cause me concern. While "normal" people saw a photograph as it exists, I saw (and focused on) all the distortions and highlights of the photograph's negative. It was the best way I knew to describe how utterly distorted my perception of my surroundings had become.

The doctor listened intently and asked me questions about my life—my childhood, my high school and college experiences, my family life, my career, and, of course, any drug or alcohol use, and whether I had ever thought about suicide. In response to the question on suicide, I told him that I had never thought about suicide prior to having my present issues. And even with my issues, up to that point, I never actually considered committing suicide. It had gotten to the point, though, that thoughts had repeatedly entered my head that suggested that ending it all might be better than the embarrassment, anguish, and pain I was feeling. I knew deep in my heart that life was too precious and my family was too precious to choose anything but seeking help.

He asked if I thought there was anything in my past that might be related to the issues I was experiencing or whether anyone in my family had similar issues. I couldn't remember anyone in my family going through what I was going through. My mom worried a bit, but not excessively. My past? Generally speaking, and as far as I was concerned, my upbringing and my educational years were quite normal. In fact, I had very fond memories from my childhood. Nevertheless, as I thought about it in the psychiatrist's office that day, I did recall a few negative memories about my childhood that—if they didn't shape my outlook on life—caused me to vow that my children would never experience those things. Whether the events behind those memories had anything to do with my OCD, I'm not sure. I do know, however, that they had an impact on me. To understand the relevance or significance of these memories, it's helpful to have a little background.

Growing Up

I grew up in High Ridge, Missouri—a small town on the outskirts of the St. Louis metropolitan area. I was one of five children, the second youngest and the only boy. We were fairly close in age. Only seven years separated oldest from youngest. We were the "5 S's"—Sheri, Sandy, Sue, Shannon, and Stacy. I had a speech impediment as a child for which I had to see a speech therapist. Ironically, my impediment was a lisp, and the only letter in the alphabet that I couldn't say correctly was S. My four sisters spoiled me. I had a close relationship with them growing up and I'm close with them today. They are all beautiful, compassionate, and selfless human beings.

I was fairly athletic and a good student. Although I was neither the best athlete nor the best student at any level, I was driven. I worked hard and I enjoyed being involved in extracurricular activities. I also felt natural being out in front. At Northwest High in House Springs, I was a captain on the wrestling and football teams, and I was the president of my class and then the president of the student council. Academically, I graduated in the top 2 percent of my class. I went to Southwest Missouri State University, where I wrestled and then graduated cum laude with a Bachelor of Science. At the University of Missouri-Columbia School of Law, I served as the president of the Student Bar Association and made the dean's list. I can't explain all the reasons why I was driven to try to excel, but I am confident part of it stemmed from wanting to climb out of the economic conditions I experienced as a child. I do know that I wanted to make my parents proud. More than that, though, I was always conscious of not disappointing them.

Financially speaking, we were very poor during my childhood. But as kids, we really didn't know anything different and we never talked about ourselves as being poor. We survived in large part because we were a tight-knit family and focused more on what we had than what we didn't have. My parents insisted that we work hard in school, stay out of trouble, do our chores, show respect to adults, be honest, and be sensitive to the feelings of others. If there was an emphasis, it was on honesty and being sensitive to the feelings of others. If any of us told a lie or said anything remotely hurtful to anyone (particularly one of the other siblings), the offender would be in *big* trouble.

We were also close with our extended family. I always looked forward to the major holidays because it meant we were with our grandparents, uncles and aunts, and cousins. That was always a blast! We were very tight with our neighbors too. Even though none of the neighbors were related, all the kids in the neighborhood addressed the adults as "Uncle" or "Aunt" followed by the first name. The kids played outside nearly all the time, no matter the weather conditions. I can still hear all the moms in the neighborhood yelling at the top of their lungs for their respective children to come home for supper at the end of the day.

Growing up, our house seemed to be a magnet for many of the neighbors. There was always something happening at our house. There was a lot of laughter, music, and sports on the television or radio. (I still have fond memories of listening to Jack Buck and Mike Shannon call Cardinal baseball.) We also had tons of pets. At one point we had twenty-eight cats (all outside), five dogs (all inside), a rabbit, a skunk, and two doves. There was never a dull moment in our house and rarely a quiet one.

While my dad certainly loved us and tried to instill a good set of values in us, it was really my mom who was the "glue" that held the family together. My mom (Gertrude or "Trudy" Shy) had a high school education and worked as a typesetter once I started first grade. She was easy to talk to, had a great sense of humor, became involved in her children's school and youth sport activities, and served as a confidant to many of her children's friends. She made every holiday and birthday special and memorable.

As I mentioned earlier, she worried, but not excessively. Like most mothers, she was convinced that we would all get polio if we stepped in a mud puddle. Now and then, she would ask if any of us kids smelled "something burning," but to be honest, her concerns weren't misplaced. We had a "fire-breathing" furnace that sounded like a bundle of dynamite exploding and spewed fire when it turned on. You never really knew whether the furnace was going to heat the house by the traditional method of warm air flowing through the vents or simply by the bonfire method. Once, when my dad was away, my mom smelled "something burning" in the middle of the night but couldn't find the cause. She did what any rational mother would do—she called the fire department, scared the you-know-what out of us, and made us kids get all the clothes out of the house. Among a throng of curious and concerned neighbors adorned in bathrobes and pajamas, and just before the firemen put their axes into the walls, the fire chief reported that our "fire" was a burned-out tube in the television!

Outside of worrying about a polio epidemic during the spring rainy season and the house going up in a ball of fire, the most I saw her worry is when she was a passenger in a car. She was quite adept at slamming on those invisible brakes and turning around to look out of the rear window. She didn't want to witness the crash that was sure to happen as the car 500 feet in front us put on its brakes. A tragedy to all who knew her, she passed away at age forty-six in 1984 after a short bout with cancer (a few weeks before my twenty-first birthday). I still miss her. I often think of her in terms of being a guardian angel.

My dad (Albert or "Al" Shy) was a proud, stubborn, hard-working, and honest man who would give anyone in need the shirt off his back. An Army veteran of six years after dropping out of high school, he earned a living as an auto mechanic, a business owner, and then later as a salesman. He was physically strong, had a quick wit, and possessed an analytical mind. Resourceful and mechanically inclined, he could build and fix anything. You wouldn't believe the number of applications a coat hanger and duct tape have! He was really a big kid at heart. He loved to hunt and fish, drive fast on curvy, dangerous roads, rev the car engine at stoplights and in the driveway, and go to stock car races. Being able to "lay rubber" in second gear gave him a tremendous sense of satisfaction and pleasure (even at age sixty)!

When I was a young boy, he was my Superman. I respected no one more than I respected my dad. As the only boy, I had a special relationship with my dad. He taught me how to hunt and fish, "let" me help him work on cars, let me go to work with him at the gas station (I had a mechanic's shirt that said "Little Al"), and was my biggest fan when I played football and wrestled. I've got a plethora of great memories and funny stories of my experiences with my dad. I remember him telling me he was proud of me four times in my life—when I graduated college, when I was commissioned a Marine officer, when I graduated law school, and when I was ten years old.

The incident when I was ten occurred on the way home from school on the last day before Christmas vacation. The weather changed for the worst quickly and our bus got stuck on the icy back roads of High Ridge. We were about two miles from my subdivision. Although it would never happen today, our bus driver asked me (the fifth grader and oldest kid on the bus) to take ten to fifteen younger kids who lived in my subdivision home. The driver took care of the remaining kids and the bus. I escorted the kids through the snowy woods and delivered each to his or her doorstep. One of the neighbors, whose first-grade son I had given a candy cane to because he lost his on the walk home, called my dad at work to tell him what I had done. My dad telephoned me at my friend's house and said, "Son, you just did a very brave thing getting all those kids home. I couldn't be more proud." I stood on top of the world that day because of that phone call.

Of course, like other parents, my dad also made stuff up about me to make me sound more interesting. He was convinced (and told everyone) that I was the youngest Marine to be promoted to Major in the history of the Marine Corps. No matter how many times I attempted to "correct the record," he absolutely would not accept the fact that it wasn't true.

My dad was quite the character. He was short in stature and compensated for it with a certain degree of machismo. Some call it "short man's complex." Indeed, the degree of macho-ness seemed to be directly proportional to how much taller a man was than my dad. Other than an irrational fear of snakes (even a tiny non-poisonous snake would suffer a violent death at the hands of my father), my dad did not openly worry about anything and didn't appear to fear anyone or anything. He took no bull from anyone—employee, co-worker, boss, teacher, school principal, or man driving down the road. Regarding the latter, if another man cut him off while driving (even if it was my dad's fault to begin with), my dad would make it clear to the other driver that the conflict could immediately be settled by pulling over. This always caused my mom great grief.

He had a definite opinion on what it meant to be a man. He evaluated the character of a man in part by the firmness of his handshake. He evaluated toughness by punching you in the arm and seeing if you winced. It was rare that my friends and I were able to walk into a room with my dad in it and not receive a good solid punch in the arm from him. He wasn't being mean. I actually think it was a form of "hello" for him.

He had little respect for men who were not tough physically or emotionally, or as he saw it, "weak." What my friends today call the "line of the century" will give you some idea of how my dad saw the world (at least the entire time I knew him). In 1991, at age fifty-five, my dad had a massive heart attack. I was called home on emergency leave from Okinawa, Japan. After ten days in intensive care, the doctors released him. The next day, my dad asked me to drive him to his work. It was a freezing cold February day in St. Louis. While in his house, I handed him his coat, but he refused to wear it. After arguing with him and tossing the coat back and forth, I finally relented and we went outside. His neighbor was working outside, bundled up like an Eskimo. I said to my dad, "You see, at least he knows that when it's freezing outside, sensible people wear a coat." Without missing a beat, and as serious as he could be, my dad replied, "Son, I'm not going to let this heart attack turn me into a wussy." (Except he didn't say "wussy.") I didn't know how to respond to that except to say, "Dad, I don't know how to respond to that."

My dad was the most resilient man I have ever met. When I was a baby, a car that he was lying underneath fell off of the jack and crushed one side of his face. Adrenaline helped him lift the car off. He then walked into the house holding the side of his face and calmly asked my mom for a towel. Doctors reconstructed his face. In his late thirties, a trash truck fell on his leg when the hydraulic lift lost pressure and came crashing down. That incident left a scar from his ankle to his hip. Finally, when he was in his mid-forties, he was hit by a car and dragged for about one hundred yards. Some man, angry at one of my dad's friends, was outside of a bar and drove his car at the crowd of people in which my dad and his friend were standing. My dad, like everyone else in that crowd, tried to jump out of the way of the car. The car swerved at the last second and hit my dad. My dad grabbed on to the front bumper after the car hit him. He was dragged over asphalt and gravel and finally let go when the car bounced in and out of a large depression in the asphalt. His pelvis was broken and about 50 percent of the skin on his back had been ripped away. He was hospitalized for six weeks, underwent major skin graft surgery, and had to learn how to walk again.

My dad lived another seven years after his heart attack. It was cancer that finally brought him to his knees. He died in 1998 at age sixty-two. I still miss him as well.

As much as I love my dad and revered him as a young boy, I came to realize as I grew older that he sometimes made poor, rash decisions that adversely affected our family. It is neither my intent to disrespect my dad nor to blame him for anything. I freely admit that I have made many poor decisions. To understand who I am, though, one must understand this piece of my childhood.

These poor, rash decisions sometimes resulted in my dad quitting jobs and being out of work for stretches at a time. Often these poor, rash decisions were related to my dad's stubbornness, pride, and unwillingness to tolerate what he considered to be "B.S." from a boss. There were also times when he and Mom would argue and he would get angry and simply move out. When he was working, we didn't have much money. When he wasn't working, times were definitely tough. Nonetheless, we always managed to get by. My mom relied upon food stamps, and my grandparents chipped in to make sure we had the essentials. With all of this as background, I can better discuss my "negative" memories.

Due to the financial situation, bills would not get paid and the house and yard were neglected. This led to unsanitary conditions. I remember two situations that used to cause me to close my eyes and wish that the world would turn inside out so the filth would just fall away.

First, in the battle of financial priorities, the garbage bill was always the first to get the "we'll pay it next month" axe. Weeks turned into months and months to years. All the while, we stacked our trash against the back of the house. I remember rotten, smelly, decomposing trash being stacked as high as our roof, at least twenty feet deep and twenty feet wide, right next to the back door and the patio. In the summer, the stench was suffocating. The sight and the smell were embarrassing.

Second, for many years our septic tank was broken and leaked. Raw sewage would bubble up to the surface in the front yard and flow. My parents had no money to fix it. We dug a six-inch-wide trench along the sidewalk and along the driveway. For years and years, our sewage-flowing trench emptied into a ditch in front of the house. Visitors to the house were warned to watch their step. From childhood to our teenage years, we had friends (including significant others) who we had to steer around the trench. I remember one time my uncle Shannon (my mom's brother and the person I was named after) visited from Arizona. He was a vice president of an ice company, and by my estimation then, was a zillionaire. When he arrived at the house, he got out of his car and immediately stepped in the sewage trench. He ruined his shoe and a pair of pants. My mom was so embarrassed she cried. I simply wanted the world to turn inside out so the trash and sewage would fall away.

The other negative memory that changed my outlook came from an incident when I was eleven. I had stayed the night at a friend's. When I returned the following day to my house, my dad greeted me at the door and led me forcefully upstairs to the main part of the house, holding my elbow. Several of his friends from his service station were visiting. In front of this audience and without telling me what I had done, he made me bend over and place my hands on the seat of a kitchen chair that I immediately noticed had been charred by fire. In dramatic fashion (but not hard), he proceeded to repeatedly kick me in the butt while talking about how disappointed he was because of how irresponsible I had been. His friends were laughing at the spectacle.

Completely embarrassed and confused, I stood up and asked him what I had done. He pointed to the chair and told me that I had left it front of the furnace. The foam on the seat of the chair had ignited when the furnace spewed its fire. He said fortunately he had been home and it happened before everyone went to bed. Otherwise, he said that I would have burned the house down and probably would have killed our family. I was angry at myself because I disappointed my dad and I did do something irresponsible. I was angry at my dad for the public humiliation. Even then I thought that I deserved to be punished, but I didn't deserve the humiliation. The notion that I almost burned the house down and could have killed my family rattled me to my core. I got over it and moved on, but I never forgot it.

Back in the Psychiatrist's Office

The Navy psychiatrist asked me to come back the following day. I asked again if he wanted my list. He replied, "No" with an understanding smile. While I was still worried that my career was about to end, the doctor's calm, reassuring, and compassionate demeanor was comforting. I had the odd sensation of being both relieved (that I had taken this step) and in great fear (that I was no longer going to be able to provide for my family).

CHAPTER 5

THE DIAGNOSIS

"You're the One Who Asked Someone with OCD to Review Your Report"

The following day, I went back to see the psychiatrist. He handed me his four-page typed diagnosis. He explained that he had concluded I had obsessive-compulsive disorder, a severe case. The diagnosis did not surprise me, as I had suspected for some time that I actually had OCD. He told me that it would be a good idea if I read his report, right then, because of my protestations about psychiatry and quick diagnoses to "validate the profession." I initially said that I didn't need to read it. He insisted, however, so I read it.

In the report, the doctor summarized much of the information that I had given to him the day before. As I read the report, I made two observations. First, seeing all of my symptoms in print (page after page) really brought the severity of my case home to me. *I guess I really should be diagnosed with OCD.* That was the effect the doctor was looking for when he told me to read his report. Secondly, I noticed that the doctor didn't get some of the details right and didn't include much of what I had told him. *Was he not fully listening?* This caused me concern and I let him know about it. He quickly defended himself, explaining that he was trying to capture the "general" gist of what I had told him. At that point, relying on humor to pull me through a tough situation (a technique that served my family well when I was a kid), I quipped, "Hey, you're the one who asked a person with OCD to review your report." We laughed, but I was scared. I believed that the doctor had just officially confirmed that my career was over, that I was unemployable, and my family would be destroyed. I was wrong!

The doctor gave me a general explanation of OCD. My "take away" was basically that a person with OCD experiences irrational, intrusive, bizarre, and sometimes horrific thoughts (e.g., that bump was my car hitting a person). The thoughts become one's focus. Generally speaking, these thoughts cause anxiety to the person thinking them. In response to the thoughts, a person has a compulsion to act (e.g., turn the car around to see if you actually hit a person with your car) to quell the anxiety. Until the person takes the action in response to the thought, the body reacts physically (e.g. stomach pains, sweating, increased heart rate, pounding heartbeat; hot flashes). Once the person *caves* and performs the compulsive act, the anxiety and body's physical reactions subside—for the moment, that is. The more one gives in to the compulsive act, the stronger and more frequent the thoughts become, and proportionately, the stronger the compulsive urges become, and in turn, the physical symptoms. Hence the endless loop feeds upon itself. The doctor indicated that giving in to the compulsion was analogous to throwing gas on a fire.

He pointed out that OCD was a rather common disorder (millions of people suffer from it) and it affected people in different ways. He said OCD is different than Obsessive-compulsive Personality Disorder (OCPD), which is much more common and less severe. He mentioned that people with OCPD may, for example, constantly clean the house (even when it doesn't need it) or require that everything be neat or organized. He also pointed out that many professionals, such as doctors and lawyers, and other high-achievers have traces of OCD. In fact, he said, it helps them do their jobs. *Okay, that's a good thing, I guess.*

Most importantly for me, he said that he would be "laughed out of the psychiatric profession" if he concluded that I was "unfit for duty" just because I had OCD. He did say that had I not taken steps to begin addressing the problem, my OCD would have eventually made me unfit for duty. I had never been more relieved in my life. I wasn't going to lose my career. I was still employable. My family wouldn't be destroyed.

I recall the doctor explaining to me that the medical profession was not yet certain what caused OCD. He mentioned the possibility that heredity and one's experiences and environment may contribute to OCD. However, he explained the prevailing view was that OCD was linked to communications in the brain and a deficiency of a chemical called serotonin. He indicated there were medications designed to regulate or increase serotonin levels. The medication, he said, helps lessen or weaken OCD's symptoms. As I recall, the doctor was doubtful that anything in my past or genes contributed to my OCD. Yet, he neither discounted nor discarded the possibility.

Remember, I'm not a medical doctor and this isn't medical advice. Consult your own competent medical sources, including your doctor, for an explanation about the cause or causes of OCD. I will note that still today it appears, from this layman's perspective, that the medical profession is not in complete agreement about the potential causes of OCD.

For treatment he prescribed a combination of medication (fluvoxamine, a selective serotonin reuptake inhibitor called Luvox) and behavioral therapy. He didn't really say too much about the behavioral therapy at this time, except that it would be with a psychologist. He indicated that while the behavioral therapy was necessary, he needed to get a baseline on the effectiveness of the medication. Thus, he said he wanted to wait one month before I started behavioral therapy. Being the good patient, I simply nodded in agreement. However, in a few weeks I would be back in his office, urgently asking that I start behavioral therapy immediately so I had some tools to help me address my issues.

CHAPTER 6

THE FIRST FEW WEEKS AFTER DIAGNOSIS
The Bottom of the Bottom

With my diagnosis in hand, I immediately did two things. First, I told my closest friends, my boss, my sisters, and of course, my wife, that I had been diagnosed with OCD. Since I felt that they had begun thinking of me as an odd person due to my unusual behaviors, I wanted them all to know that there was a physical medical cause at the root and that I wasn't "weird" or "crazy." I received tremendous support from them all. Almost all of them told me that they thought it was courageous for me to address the issue. My boss gave me as much flexibility as I needed during the workday to do what I deemed necessary. For example, the Luvox made me sleepy, so he let me close my office door and doze off whenever I felt the need. This support network and the encouragement these folks provided were instrumental in my recovery. They were nonjudgmental and gave me the room to get better.

I also had the urge to tell others of my OCD affliction, including Marine Corps leadership at the base and some of my clients. I felt it was important that they know that I wasn't "weird" or "crazy." The same officer who used to tease me about trash (still a close friend and now a senior executive) advised me not to make these disclosures. He made this recommendation because he was not sure how they might use or evaluate such information. Also, recognizing my apparent desire to broadcast my newly diagnosed disorder far and wide, he thought that it was important for me to maintain some sense of privacy about my medical condition. He drove this point home by bluntly remarking, "It's none of their goddamned business."

The frankness of his delivery got my attention and had an immediate impact. It helped me (and continues to help me) sort out to whom, when, and how I should disclose my information. I stopped telling people I had been diagnosed with OCD. As much as I wanted to let everyone know that I was behaving oddly due to OCD, I realized I didn't need to explain away my behavior. I concluded at that point that it wasn't important for the general public to know that I had OCD. Although I was concerned that others might be judgmental, I decided initially not to disclose my condition because my privacy *was* important to me and I really just wanted to focus on getting better.

As I worked my way through behavioral therapy, which I will discuss shortly, I added two reasons for not disclosing my condition. First, as I explain better in the next chapter, part of my behavioral strategy was for me to treat OCD as a separate entity. I did not want to disclose that I had OCD because I did not want anyone to associate OCD as being part of me. Second, as I learned that I could manage my OCD, my objective became to manage OCD in such a way that people would never guess that I had OCD. (In fact, one of the best compliments I receive now after I do disclose my diagnosis is "I had no idea you have OCD.")

As a result of that blunt advice I received back in 1997, I have disclosed my diagnosis under three conditions: 1) when filling out official paperwork asking if I have any mental disorders; (e.g., medical questionnaires, security clearance questionnaires); 2) when I feel like I can help someone who I suspect might have OCD; and, most recently 3) in relation to this book.

As mentioned in chapter 1, the second thing I did after my diagnosis was to go to a bookstore and start reading about OCD. Unfortunately, because I didn't yet have any tools to manage the thoughts that OCD was now *catapulting* into my mind with rapid-fire speed, reading about OCD wasn't helpful to me. The first book about OCD that I picked up stated up front that OCD was not curable. My doctor told me on my next visit that the statement technically may be true but it needs some context. He explained that there was no magical cure, but offered that if you learn to manage OCD through behavioral therapy—and I can now attest to this—you can lead a virtually symptom-free life and can even get to the point where you feel like you are cured. I accepted the answer, although somewhat circumspectly. I eventually learned, however, through my own personal journey that the doctor was 100 percent correct. For my own purposes, I took the doctor's assessment one step further and simply redefined the word "cure" as it applied to me.

Reading the "incurable" passage was demoralizing, but it wasn't devastating. Because of the *power of suggestion* (which my doctor told me later is common in OCD patients) reading about others' symptoms devastated me. At the bookstore, on a bright, sunny Saturday morning in Jacksonville, North Carolina, I read that some people with OCD have thoughts about committing violent acts against children. I recoiled, both emotionally and physically, when I read this. *I have never had thoughts about committing violence on a child! I could never have such thoughts! I love children. I have children! I won't allow myself to have those thoughts!* You can predict what was about to happen. Trying to resist a thought or attempting to *not think* a thought is futile in the cruel world of OCD.

I left the bookstore horrified. As I drove home from the bookstore, all I did was try *not* to think about my children, and more specifically, try not to think violent thoughts about my children. Consequently, OCD filled my mind with thoughts about hitting my kids. It actually got to the point during that short drive home where I told myself that I was going to have to either call the police (to report myself for something I had not done) or commit suicide. When I got home from the bookstore that morning, I intended to simply avoid my children. As I came through the front door and was heading to the garage, my five-year-old son, who had heard the car pull up and the front door open, called me back to the "toy room" where he and his one-year-old brother were playing. My wife was in the hallway next to the toy room.

I saw the one-year-old first and tried only to think beautiful thoughts about him. Then, suddenly and much to my horror, I envisioned myself walking up to him as he played on the floor and kicking him in the head. I then immediately thought of doing the same thing to the five-year-old. I darted out of the room. Distraught, I urgently called to my wife. She knew something was wrong from the sound of my voice. I told her that I needed to leave the house and get a hotel room. I explained what I had read in the bookstore and what I had just thought about seeing myself do to the kids. She gave me a hug and told me that I wasn't going anywhere. She said she knew in her heart that I would never do anything to harm the kids and that this was just my OCD. She said she was there to help me through this. She told me I needed to talk to the doctor about what happened. I wasn't scheduled to see the doctor for a month, but I called and made an appointment for that Monday.

My wife's support that day was not only critical and helpful, given the unnerved and despondent state I found myself in, it became a cornerstone in my recovery. She was able to recognize and believe that my thoughts about harming our children were OCD thoughts and not *my* thoughts. She recognized that these thoughts were completely inconsistent with my character and counter to who I was as a person and a father. Because of this, she had confidence that I had no intention of carrying these thoughts out. As I progressed in my behavioral therapy, I not only thought of her support on this day with appreciation, but her ability to characterize the OCD thoughts as not being *my* thoughts was very useful to me. *If she could do it, I could do it.*

I saw the doctor the next Monday. We talked about keeping the term "cure" in its proper context, and we talked about the power of suggestion and the problem with trying to resist an OCD thought. He didn't want the behavioral therapy to start yet, however. He advised me to hold off on the therapy to let the medicine take effect first. The downward spiral did not stop there.

A few weeks later, I had officer-of-the-day duty at the base. During the evening, I received a phone call from a young Marine who sounded like he had been drinking and was depressed. I talked to him for a while and explained to him that I would get him some help. I got his name, barracks and room number, unit, and the name of his squad leader. After I hung up with the Marine, I immediately called the duty chaplain and his squad leader, asking both of them to go check on the Marine and then notify me when they had done so. They said they would. The chaplain indicated to me that he was going to have the young man taken to the hospital. I hung up the phone and felt good that I had taken steps to help this Marine. Then my OCD kicked in.

He said something about killing himself. What? No he didn't. He said he was homesick and he didn't have any friends. No, he said he wanted to kill himself. My stomach turned and I got a hot flash. *Oh Jesus, I need to inform the chaplain and his squad leader that he said he was going to kill himself. No, he didn't say he was going to kill himself.* I won't go through the sordid details, but suffice it to say that I called the chaplain several times that night, trying to explain that I didn't think the young Marine had said anything about suicide but maybe I misheard him. I couldn't sleep that night.

By the following day, I had become non-functional. I lay on the floor in my office, trying to sleep, but the thought of that young Marine killing himself sent me into dark depths. The Marine officer who had originally encouraged me to seek help about my "odd" behaviors noticed that I was *really* distraught and asked me what was going on. I told him about the young Marine and the violent thoughts with my kids. I told him about the medication and the doctor's decision to delay behavioral therapy. He suggested I talk to the psychiatrist and ask for some advice on how to deal with OCD besides relying just on medication. I needed some tools.

I called the hospital and said I needed to see my doctor that day. I was told he was out. I insisted that I see someone. I was seen that day by another Navy Lieutenant. I told him about the Marine I encountered while on duty and the violent thoughts about my sons. With regard to the Marine, I insisted that he ensure that the Marine was okay and to confirm whether the Marine had said something about killing himself. He said that if they had brought the Marine in to the emergency room, the doctors would have discovered whether he had suicidal ideations or tendencies. He told me that I had done what I was supposed to do as officer-of-the-day and that I could let it go. (Once I had told the doctor, a person in a position of psychiatric responsibility over the Marine, I was able to let it go.) With regard to my sons, he explained that the consequence I experienced after "trying not to think the thought" was a classic OCD symptom and that it didn't mean I really wanted to hurt my children. He made an appointment for me with my regular doctor and said he would recommend to him that I start behavioral therapy immediately.

CHAPTER 7

BEHAVIORAL THERAPY

"The Chinese Finger Trap" and Developing a Strategy

My psychologist was also a Navy Lieutenant. Like my psychiatrist, he was calm and reassuring, and gave me the impression of being wise and mature beyond his years. I received behavioral therapy with this doctor for seven months until I transferred to the Pentagon in May 1998. Those seven months were a blur. My therapy wasn't just sitting in his office for thirty minutes every couple weeks. Therapy was an intense 24/7 endeavor.

In my first session with the doctor, he provided an analogy that helped explain the consequences of resisting an OCD intrusive irrational thought. I use this analogy even today when explaining how OCD works. To illustrate the point of "the more one resists an OCD thought, the stronger the thought becomes," he used the analogy of the phenomenon associated with the Chinese finger trap, a woven, flexible cylinder device barely larger than one's fingers. The object of the finger trap is to place each index finger into each end of the cylinder then try to remove your fingers. If you simply pull your index fingers apart, the trap will constrict and your fingers will be "trapped." The harder you pull, the tighter the cylinder gets. Instead, if you relax and "go with" the trap by pushing your fingers together and slowly twisting out, the trap releases the index fingers. And so it is with OCD. The more you try to resist the thought, the tighter OCD constricts you and the stronger and more intrusive the thought becomes. I learned, and in time, mastered the tool of simply accepting the thought; going with the flow. I incorporated this tool into my behavioral therapy.

My psychologist was of the opinion that behavioral therapy was key to successful long-term management of OCD. He agreed that medication appeared to be helpful in relieving symptoms, but his focus was on the behavioral approach to treating OCD. At the time, I boiled his advice down to this: *Identify the intrusive, irrational thought as an OCD thought. Do not resist the thought; resist the compulsion.* The advice was relatively straightforward, and as he indicated, was basically consistent with the behavioral approach used in the profession to treat OCD. Thinking back, I don't remember the doctor giving me any special behavioral exercises to implement the advice between visits. He might have; I don't know. I don't think it would have mattered to me anyway. I didn't need special exercises. There were more than enough obsessions and compulsions from my office to my house and everywhere in between to give me sufficient practice. Again, therapy was an intense 24/7 endeavor.

While the doctor's advice may have been straightforward, putting it into practice in *my* OCD world wasn't. It wasn't that the advice was bad or wrong. It was great advice. I just had to mold it to fit me. Through repeated trial and error, by "falling" and "getting back up" time and again, by fretting over thoughts and caving to compulsions (and then feeling guilty about it), I finally settled upon a strategy that worked for me. I changed my perspective a bit; incorporated a couple of simple phrases that have always quietly given me comfort, confidence, courage, and hope; and stayed true to the strategy.

In time, I began to think of my strategy in terms of "Ground Rules" and "Checkpoints." I developed five Ground Rules and six Checkpoints. Implementing the Ground Rules resulted in successful management of my OCD. The Checkpoints helped me implement the Ground Rules. The next chapter sets forth the Ground Rules and Checkpoints in a way that I hope will make sense to the reader and show I how used them. Before I lay out the strategy, however, it may be useful for me to explain how I developed the Ground Rules and Checkpoints using the psychologist's basic advice as my starting point.

1. Identify the intrusive, irrational thought as an OCD thought. Conceptually, this piece of advice was difficult to wrap my brain around. The idea is rather simple—when you have an intrusive, irrational thought, characterize it as an OCD thought. Once you know you are dealing with an OCD thought, you are in a better position to implement the other parts of the behavioral response. Easy enough? Not for me. Initially, I became frustrated because I didn't know how to differentiate what was an intrusive, irrational thought and what was a thought about a legitimate issue with which I needed to be concerned. All the thoughts seemed to be about legitimate issues. *Why would I become anxious and then get adverse physical reactions about issues if I didn't think they were legitimate issues?*

I worked through this dilemma in phases and adopted a couple of different techniques. Initially, my psychologist helped me figure out what should have been obvious to me: It is an OCD thought if it causes me to second guess what I see or hear, that makes me anxious, and that causes an adverse physical reaction (e.g., hot flashes, increased heart rate) while I debate whether to take some action in response. Said in another way, "if you're experiencing the symptoms of OCD, you know it is OCD." This initial approach was beneficial and a good place to start. It took the guesswork out of the equation. Each time I went through the anguish and pain and identified a thought as OCD, I gained information to be stored and relied upon later. I was creating a mental database of OCD thoughts.

Nevertheless, although it was a good place to start, identifying an OCD thought *after* I had experienced the anguish and the pain wasn't my ultimate objective. My objective was to be able to identify the OCD thought *before* the anguish and the pain. Moreover, the "after-the-fact" technique didn't always work. There were many times when I believed the "thought" was an

OCD thought, but my OCD convinced me otherwise. This was particularly true for intrusive thoughts that I had not experienced before. For example, after I started my therapy, I started getting thoughts in church that I was on the verge of standing up and yelling that everyone in the congregation was a fake follower of Jesus, or on other occasions, that there was no God. (This was a delayed *power of suggestion* symptom I encountered from my brief perusal of a book the morning after my diagnosis.) These thoughts were absolutely contrary to my faith and my firmly held beliefs. Talk about being distraught and feeling guilty! Also, while walking in crowded public places (such as the mall), I started envisioning myself walking up to people and punching them in the face. The compulsion with both of these types of intrusive, irrational thoughts was to leave the church or public place to be sure I wouldn't do something stupid.

I started thinking that OCD was deliberately trying to stay one step ahead of me. It was like I was in a "cat-and-mouse" game and OCD was trying to outsmart me. *Am I ever going to get over this?!* Two interesting phenomena (for lack of a better word) flowed from thinking about OCD in this context. First, I began thinking very naturally about OCD as something separate and independent from me; a separate entity. This seemed kind of odd to me, so I didn't know initially whether this was good or bad for my recovery. *Am I schizophrenic?!* However, I went with the flow, as I remembered reading in one of the books I perused early on that some OCD patients think of OCD in this way. I began thinking about OCD almost like it was another person, although I never actually gave my OCD "person" status. I just thought of my OCD as something with its own separate identity. I started thinking to myself, *I'm not OCD and OCD is not me.* It turns out, in my case, that thinking of OCD in this fashion *was* a good thing. It became easier for me to deal with OCD if it was disconnected from me.

Second, I began thinking naturally of my efforts to manage OCD as a contest or a battle. In this regard, I realized that OCD (the separate entity) was trying to ruin my life. OCD was trying to hurt me and my family. OCD wanted nothing more than to make my life miserable. OCD was trying to defeat me. I began thinking of OCD as my enemy. This perspective became an effective tool for me in my fight against OCD, so much so that it became an independent Ground Rule.

This perspective also caused me to tweak the psychologist's advice a bit. Rather than just identifying the thought as OCD, I found it helpful to also attribute the thought to its rightful owner (the separate entity called OCD). I changed "*identify* the intrusive, irrational thought as an OCD thought" to "Identify the thought as an intrusive, irrational thought and attribute the thought to its rightful owner, OCD." *They weren't my thoughts and I wasn't going to accept ownership of them. I'm not OCD and OCD is not me.*

My new perspective gave me something (some *thing*) to which I could affix the intrusive thoughts, but it still didn't solve the mystery behind the determination of whether a thought was "intrusive and irrational" or about an issue of legitimate concern. The final phase of thought identification and attribution involved the Socratic method of learning. *After all, I am a lawyer and I did minor in philosophy in college.* Reflecting on the types of questions both my psychiatrist and my psychologist asked me about the intrusive, irrational thoughts (which I presume were designed to get me to examine the thoughts in a rational manner), I started asking myself questions to help me pinpoint whether the thoughts were of OCD origin. "Do you think that might be an OCD thought? Do you believe you would actually do something like that? Would you consider that to be a rational thought or an irrational thought? How so?" If it was a particularly relentless thought, the self-questioning could be exhaustive. For example: "Do you normally check the coffeepot or lock the door before you leave? Do you normally leave the coffeepot on or the door unlocked after you check it? Is it rational to think that you didn't check it properly? Is it rational to think that the coffeepot turned itself back on or the door unlocked itself? You are a rational person. OCD is not rational. Do you think that it is possible that OCD wants you to believe that the coffeepot may still be on or that that the door is unlocked?"

With my new perspective, I got fairly adept at spotting the OCD thought. My Checkpoint became: *This is an intrusive, irrational thought. OCD is at it again. I am a rational person. OCD is irrational and wants me to have its irrational thought.* As I progressed in my therapy, I could simply think to myself,

OCD is at it again, and then I could move on to the next Ground Rule and Checkpoint. Ultimately—and this is the great news for you—there became a point in my management of OCD where I would have an OCD thought, tell myself it was an OCD thought, and *THAT WOULD BE THE END OF IT. ALL OF IT. NO COMPULSION. NO PAIN. NO NOTHING!*

2. Do not resist the thought. Starting with the "violence against children" thoughts, I had already had considerable experience with this piece of advice. I understood the advice and I understood the consequence of resisting. The problem was, the advice only told me what *not* to do. It didn't suggest what I should do. I struggled for several months. I spent a lot of time thinking about the Chinese finger trap analogy and it finally made sense to me. For me, the meaning of the analogy was more than just "don't resist." It also had specific direction to "go with the flow." In the context of these intrusive thoughts, "going with the flow" translated into *allow the thought to be in your mind.* My Ground Rule became: *Allow the intrusive, irrational thought. Do not resist the thought.*

Implementing this Ground Rule was difficult. OCD was the master trickster and would often attempt to confuse me by telling me that the real reason I was allowing a particular thought is because I enjoyed having the thought. (Remember when I said that OCD is relentless?) Further, many of the thoughts were despicable, horrifying, or downright grotesque. They ran counter to the core of my very being and I didn't want them in my head. Finally, by enduring a lot of grief and through the development of various techniques, I learned how to allow the thoughts. One technique I used when OCD presented me with an intrusive, irrational thought was indifference. I would tell myself, "I don't care whether this thought is in my head or not." Generally, I followed this with another technique of picturing myself *moving out of the way* and allowing the thought to come into my mind. It didn't matter if it was the most repulsive thought I could ever imagine. I let it in. I would tell myself such things as: "I am a compassionate human being. Allowing the thought does not mean I agree with it. Thoughts never hurt anyone."

The statements above were very helpful in reassuring me that it was safe to allow the thought. But one particular word became my mantra in dealing with OCD—"okay." I'm not sure why, but the word "okay" has always signified "peace" and "balance." It is a response I give people when they ask me how I'm doing or how things are going. Taking that a step further, the statements "It's okay" and "It'll be okay" have always provided me a sense of comfort, confidence, courage, and—regarding the latter phrase—a sense of hope. I really can't point to a particular incident in my life where the word "okay" or these statements became significant to me. I just remember saying the word to describe myself when I felt at peace, and I remember using the statements to help myself or others get through stressful, difficult, or unhappy times.

As I developed my technique to *allow the thought,* the statement, "It's okay" became the anchor of my fourth Checkpoint. After attributing the intrusive, irrational thought to OCD, I would implement the "allow the thought" Ground Rule by telling myself: *I don't care whether I have this thought or not, but it's okay if I do. It's okay if this thought is in mind. Thoughts never hurt anyone. I am a compassionate person. Allowing the thought doesn't mean I agree with it, enjoy it, or believe that it's true. It's okay. It's okay. It's okay.*

Some days, I would rely upon all of these statements. Other days, simple indifference and then repeating, "It's okay" were effective. Ultimately, by the time I was off medication, I could simply say "It's okay" when an intrusive thought showed up, and I would be free and clear of the thought. Neither anxiety nor physical reactions would come into the picture. In the context of my battle against OCD, I had figured out that allowing the thought (i.e., not resisting the thought) confused my enemy, OCD. OCD's tactical objective was to get me to fret about the thought and then try to resist the thought. Resisting the thought would make OCD stronger. By allowing the thought, I took OCD's non-human *legs* out from under it.

3. Resist the compulsion. How do you resist doing the one thing that will relieve the anguish and the pain? A better question is "Why *should* you resist the one thing that will relieve the anguish and pain (and prevent the disaster from occurring)? If you believe you may have left the coffeepot on, for example, a rational, caring person would go back and check. Right? If you don't check and it *was* left on, certainly your house will burn down and your children will die in the fire. All you have to do is go back and check to make sure it is off. Any decision other than going back means you are a worthless human being. The anguish and the pain and the guilt become unbearable. You go back and check. The anguish and the pain go away. But the guilt doesn't. It is guilt experienced for a different reason (you caved and went back), but it is guilt nonetheless. Worse than that, the obsessions and compulsions have just been fueled. *They will come back. They will come back stronger and with a vengeance. That is why you must resist. If you don't resist the compulsion, you will not get better. It is that simple.*

My Ground Rule was the same as the doctor's basic advice, but I added a phrase to remind myself that the amount of pain I experienced was not relevant and repeated the word "resist" a few times for emphasis. My Ground Rule became *Resist the compulsion, no matter the pain. Resist, resist, resist!* I kept reminding myself that the second part of OCD's grand scheme to screw up my life was to compel me to respond to the intrusive, irrational thought. I told myself that I could and must resist. No matter how painful the mental anguish, no matter how tied up in knots my stomach got, no matter how much I perspired, no matter how fast my heart raced, no matter how much my enemy OCD whispered in my ear that I would be shamed and that I would be the most horrible person in the world if I did not comply with OCD's unreasonable demand that I respond, *my objective was not to respond.* I resisted. I failed many times at first. I picked myself up, dusted myself off, and tried again the next time.

Initially, I used the Socratic method to try to resist. For instance, I might ask, "Do you believe it would be helpful to go back and check? Do you believe it would be helpful to wash your hands again? Is it rational to think that the house will burn down and your kids will die if you don't go back and check the iron?" This was helpful, but it wasn't enough for me. As I progressed, I incorporated the statement that gave me comfort, confidence, courage, and hope—"It'll be okay if you don't do what OCD wants you to do."

As an aside, you might be wondering why I chose to use, "It'll be okay," here and not, "It's okay." After all, doesn't, "It'll be okay" suggest that it is not presently okay, but *will be* some time in the future? I suppose there is a point to be made with that question. However, "It'll be okay" worked for me. First, and maybe most importantly, it was purely a natural response. That's what gave me comfort, courage, and confidence. Second, the forward-looking statement was my attempt to assure myself that nothing adverse would happen if I didn't cave to the compulsion. For example, the house will not burn down and the kids won't die if I don't go back and check. Finally, in my determined battle against OCD ("epic struggle" sounds too dramatic) the statement, "It'll be okay," took on a more significant, philosophically profound meaning. I was telling myself that I was winning the battle. I was going to get better. I finally had hope that I would make it through. (And hence, why I think it is such an appropriate title for this book.)

I developed two checkpoints for Ground Rule #5 *(Resist the compulsion, no matter the pain. Resist, resist, resist!)* Checkpoint #5A was fairly basic. I would say "It'll be okay if I don't ..." That would be followed with some questions to myself. And then it would end with repeating the phrase "It'll be okay" over and over. If I was still "feeling the heat" after this, I would move on to my final stop, Checkpoint #5B. In Checkpoint #5B, I would tell myself that if it turned out I was wrong about not responding and the *horrible tragedy* that I was worrying about happened, and someone questioned me as to why I didn't respond, I would simply respond: *I have OCD and I have been told that I won't get better if I give in to this compulsion. You can do whatever you want to me, but I want to get better.* I'll save the good news about this at the end of the next chapter, where I set forth the strategy.

Apart from the Chinese finger trap analogy and the behavioral therapy, I had one final distinctive memory from my sessions with this psychologist. Near the end of my therapy with him (just before I transferred from Camp Lejeune in May 1998) and after I had been relatively successful in developing and implementing my strategy, I became concerned that I would someday mistakenly identify something about which I really should be concerned as an OCD thought. I had become fairly successful at resisting all compulsions. What if I really should take action?

I asked the psychologist what I was to do if I actually saw something that really did deserve my assistance. I used the example of driving by a lake and seeing a boat with people on it that was actually sinking. At first, he said "ignore it." I challenged him. I said, "No, I'm talking about a boat that actually is sinking." He said, "It's an OCD thought. Resist acting on it." I pressed him.

"You don't understand what I'm asking. I'm talking about seeing a real boat with real people on it that anyone, including you, not just us OCD people, would conclude that the boat was sinking. What do I do?" He said something to the effect of: "You need to resist acting on OCD thoughts and compulsions. If you actually see a boat sinking, you'll know it, and you can help them."

The advice made absolute sense to me. What I took away from that conversation was that I needed to stay true to the behavioral approach (my strategy). I became confident that I would know and act appropriately to anything that might be an actual problem, because that was in my true character. That's who I am. In my final Checkpoint, for purposes of working through OCD thoughts and compulsions, I did leave room for the slight possibility that I could be wrong, but the truth is I developed the utmost confidence that I wouldn't be wrong if I stayed true to the strategy. Philosophically, this advice and this perspective comforted me in the sense that I knew I didn't have to resist the desire or need to help people who *actually* were in distress.

I met with the Camp Lejeune doctors until I transferred to the Pentagon in May 1998. The two Navy Lieutenants were particularly helpful to me in placing the responsibility for managing my OCD on me, and for also reassuring me that I would succeed. When I transferred to the Pentagon, I saw a psychiatrist and a psychologist at the naval hospital in Bethesda, Maryland. They also were helpful, but at this point I had already figured out my system for managing my OCD, so my visits were basically tied around my medication and the need to get a prescription refill from the psychiatrist. Interestingly, I remember telling my doctors (all of them) that I didn't mind taking OCD medication for the rest of my life if it meant that I would be better. They all voiced surprise and reassured me that while medication was helpful in relieving symptoms, OCD could be managed without medication.

In September 1999, I left active duty and took a civil service job with the Department of the Navy. Although my system for managing OCD was working well, I found a civilian psychiatrist so that I could continue my medication. Notwithstanding my earlier stance of being okay with a lifetime of medication if it helped me manage OCD, within a few years, I weaned myself (with the doctor's help) off medication. Why?

Well, for starters, I had received medication from the Department of the Navy at no cost to myself for approximately two years. That, of course, changed when I left active duty. As a practical reality, I quickly figured out that I didn't like paying the amount of money I was paying for medication (even with insurance). More important than the cost of the medication, though, I learned that I could manage my OCD without medication. The success of my effort to manage my OCD through a behavioral approach resulted in me forgetting to take my medication (much like what happens when one takes antibiotics for strep throat and then forgets to take the medicine once one starts feeling better). And finally, my civilian (and final) psychiatrist was appalled by tatement that I was fine taking medication for the rest of my life. He stated emphatically that continuous medication was not always necessary to manage OCD. He then pounded his fist on his desk and stated rather angrily, "I don't know why we all think we have to be so goddamned perfect!"

What in the world was he talking about? What did managing OCD with the aid of medication have to do with perfection? And why was he so mad about it? And then, for some reason, it all clicked for me. All of the sudden, the final piece to my long-term OCD management strategy fell into place. I realized that I was trying to achieve perfection. I didn't know why. I recognized that I didn't have to be perfect and I didn't have to be perfect in my quest to manage OCD. This simple realization allowed me to summarily and confidently decide that I could manage OCD without the aid of medication. My goal became simply to manage OCD as well as Shannon Shy could do it. Working with the doctor, I weaned myself off the medication. Shortly thereafter, I stopped seeing the psychiatrist. My strategy was sound. I was no longer OCD's victim.

CHAPTER 8

THE STRATEGY

Ground Rules and Checkpoints

The following Ground Rules and Checkpoints comprised my strategy in defeating OCD. *Defeating OCD* means that I can manage OCD so I live virtually symptom-free and OCD doesn't adversely affect me. I integrated the Ground Rules into my life. They were my key to defeating OCD. I developed the Checkpoints to implement the Ground Rules. The Checkpoints were (and are, on the rare occasion I get an OCD thought these days) extremely effective for me. The words in italics are words that I said to myself. If the first Checkpoint didn't solve the issue, I moved on to the next. Ground Rules #1 and #2 were foundational for me. They persisted throughout implementation of all the Ground Rules. Usually, this meant that whenever I got an intrusive, irrational thought, I would immediately be at Ground Rule #3. I have also included some questions for Ground Rules #3 through #5, which I used to help me arrive at the Checkpoints. The Checkpoint system was a strong weapon in defeating OCD.

By following these Ground Rules and Checkpoints, the thoughts became less frequent and less intense, the compulsions became less frequent and less intense, and the physical and emotional pain associated with the thoughts and indecision about whether to act disappeared. I stayed true to them and I got better. And remember, I did not demand or expect perfection. If I caved and performed the compulsive act, I tried not to fret or feel guilty. (But if I did fret or feel guilty, I told myself "It's okay.") I tried to do better the next time. As hard as it seems, it gets easier.

Enter the Obsessive Thought...

GROUND RULE #1

Remind yourself in implementing all Ground Rules that you don't have to be perfect. The objective is to manage OCD to the best of *your* ability.

CHECKPOINT #1

I don't have to be perfect. Nobody is perfect. I'm just trying to manage OCD to the best of my ability.

GROUND RULE #2

Think of OCD as an entity separate from you. Think of OCD as your enemy and that you are in a battle to protect yourself and your family.

CHECKPOINT #2

I am not OCD. OCD is not me. OCD is trying to ruin my life. OCD wants me to be miserable. OCD is my enemy. I want to get better. I will win this battle.

GROUND RULE #3

Identify the thought as an intrusive, irrational thought and attribute the thought to its rightful owner, OCD.

CHECKPOINT #3

This is an intrusive, irrational thought. It is an OCD thought. OCD is at it again. I am a rational person. OCD is irrational and wants me to have its irrational thought.

Some Examples of Questions for Checkpoint #3

Is this an OCD thought? Would I actually do something like that?

Is that a rational or irrational thought? Why?

Is it likely I just hit somebody with my car? Is it likely that there is a person lying on the side of the road dying?

Don't I normally check that (e.g., the coffeepot or the door lock) before I leave?

If I checked it, wouldn't I normally turn it off or lock it?

Is it rational to think that I didn't check it properly or turn it off/ lock it?

Is it rational to think that the coffee pot turned itself back on or the door unlocked itself?

Isn't it most probable that OCD wants me to believe that the coffeepot may still be on or that that the door is unlocked?

Enter the Compulsion…

GROUND RULE #4

Allow the intrusive, irrational thought.

Do not resist the thought.

CHECKPOINT #4

I don't care whether I have this thought or not, but it's okay if I do. It's okay if this thought is in my mind. Thoughts never hurt anyone. I am a compassionate person. Allowing the thought doesn't mean I agree with it, enjoy it, or believe that it's true. It's okay. It's okay. It's okay.

Some Examples of Questions for Checkpoint #4

Does it matter to me whether I have this thought in my mind?

I am a rational person and OCD is irrational—Do I agree with the thought? Do I enjoy the thought?

Does the fact that the thought is in my mind mean I am going to carry out the thought?

Isn't that counter to who I am as a person?

GROUND RULE #5

RESIST the compulsion, no matter the pain! RESIST, RESIST, RESIST!

CHECKPOINT #5A

It'll be okay if I don't do what OCD wants me to do. I will not do what OCD wants me to do. I will resist. I will resist. It'll be okay if I resist and don't do what OCD wants me to do. It'll be okay. It'll be okay. It'll be okay.

Some Examples of Questions for Checkpoint #5A

Is it rational to think that all of those horrible things will really happen if I don't do what OCD wants me to do?

Will I get better if I do what OCD wants me to do?

Would it be helpful to just move on and then see what happens after I don't do what OCD wants me to do?

CHECKPOINT #5B

It'll be okay if I don't do what OCD wants me to do. If anyone ever questions me about why I didn't do what OCD wanted me to do and the horrible thing happens, I will tell them that I have OCD and I have been told that I won't get better if I give in to this compulsion. I'll tell them that they can do what they want to me, but I want to get better. It'll be okay. It'll be okay.

As promised, here's the good news ... Even though I often got to the final Checkpoint in my battle against OCD, the *horrible thing* never happened when I resisted the compulsion, and no one ever questioned me about why I didn't do what OCD wanted me to do.

CHAPTER 9

SOME HELPFUL HINTS

I am one of God's Children. I have Value. I am Loved.

There are some basic things I did that helped make my journey easier. They may be useful to you.

First, I tried to have a positive attitude. I experienced dark moments as I began my fight against OCD. Nevertheless, I tried to stay focused on why it was important to get better—my wife, my kids, my friends, my extended family, my career—and tried to look on the bright side. I had hope—hope that things would get better. Remember, this is a marathon, not a sprint. Having hope and a positive attitude are powerful lights when things get dark for you.

Second, I relied on my friends, my family, and my faith. I'm not overly religious. I do not attend church as often as I would like to or should. However, I strongly believe in God and I have an unwavering faith that Jesus Christ is my Savior. I prayed and I prayed for the strength and courage to find my way through. I also did something at church that I normally wouldn't do. (I took a risk.) When I am at church, I am somewhat private in my religious worship. I don't raise my hands and I don't hold others' hands. I don't have anything against anyone else doing it; it's just not how I am comfortable worshipping.

My normal practice of *private worship* flew right out of the window on the Sunday morning after I was diagnosed and had the violent thoughts about my kids. The pastor invited the congregation to come to the front of the church and pray with other members of the church who had been trained to reach out in prayer to those in need. Ordinarily, this is something I wouldn't do. On that day, I nearly sprinted to the front of the church and asked the team of two to pray for me in my struggle against OCD. We prayed for a long time. I told them that I needed God's help.

The prayer session genuinely *moved* me both emotionally and spiritually. With tears in my eyes, I went back to the pew where my wife was sitting. My wife was a bit surprised that I had participated in this public prayer. She never saw me do anything like that. I told her that I needed God's help and my mom's help. Through my ordeal, I was comforted and strengthened by the thought that God and my mom were by my side. I am grateful to God for healing me.

Third, I tried to enjoy life. I remembered the things that once made me happy and I went back to doing them. I got back to *living*. For example, I took my kids for walks in the woods. I took a karate class with my oldest son. I focused on family and friends.

Fourth, I continually reminded myself that I am one of God's children and I could and should love who I am. I reminded myself that I am a special part of the universe; that I have value. I reminded myself that I am loved not only by God, but also by many, many people, especially my family.

Finally, I have a couple of notes regarding alcohol. Obviously, one should follow doctor's orders regarding the consumption of alcohol while on medication and one should not use alcohol as a way to self-medicate. The consequences of violating either of these tenants could be serious and dangerous. Aside from that, in my experience, when I was learning to manage my OCD, if I had more than just one or two drinks in an evening, it was much more difficult to manage my OCD, both while under the influence and then after-the-fact.

CHAPTER 10
PARENTS AND FRIENDS
"How Can I Help?

You are a parent or a friend of someone (your loved one) who has OCD or who you think has OCD. You are probably at your wits' end about what to say or what to do. Your questions, your concerns, and your frustration are understandable. You feel bad that your loved one is suffering from these odd OCD thoughts and behaviors. You watch your loved one fret, cry, suffer, or simply shrug in embarrassment. You want to help. You want to be compassionate but you are afraid you will enable or encourage his or her behavior. You do not want to completely disengage because you do not want to seem uncaring. What do you do?!

Educate yourself about OCD. This book provides information about my experience. I highly recommend you also consult medical sources. You would be well-served to talk to a psychiatrist or a psychologist. This is in their professional lane. And remember, this book is not intended as medical advice. I can only tell you what I personally found helpful, what I believe would have been helpful (knowing what I have been through), and what was not so helpful. In that spirit, I offer the following observations.

Prior to being diagnosed with OCD, it was helpful for my wife, colleague, and sister to politely bring to my attention that they noticed something different about the way I was acting. They were not judgmental, nor did they ridicule me. My wife and my colleague both wondered if I thought I might be having some OCD symptoms. They didn't state it as a fact. It would have been unhelpful for them to play psychiatrist and attempt to diagnose me. It was helpful for my wife and colleague to encourage me to see a doctor. Although I didn't see a doctor immediately, the day I decided to call the doctor, I was comforted by the fact that others thought it was the prudent thing to do. It was consoling to know that people were concerned about me and were there to support me.

It would have been helpful for someone to tell me that he or she had done some research about OCD and discovered that there are ways to manage it in such a way that it does not adversely affect one's life. It would have been helpful for someone to tell me that having OCD doesn't mean I am "crazy" and it doesn't mean I will lose everything. It absolutely would have been unhelpful for someone to ridicule me or to put pejorative labels on me like "crazy" or "nutty."

It was helpful for the person I most relied upon for assistance, my wife, to understand that she could not be a crutch for me. It was important to have her support, but if she didn't ultimately let me be responsible for each obsessive thought or compulsion, I would not have gotten better. Before I was diagnosed, I used to ask my wife to take responsibility for checking the house and locking the door when we would leave. She used to assure me that everything would be okay when I would mention to her that something might be a problem. As I started behavioral therapy, we learned that she could no longer be that crutch. She helped me after that point by putting me on the path of making my own decisions about what to do. Initially, she would ask me a few questions about what I thought was appropriate. Eventually she got to the point where she would simply say something to the effect of "I'm here to support you 100 percent, but you'll need to figure out how to deal with that thought or whether you want to do anything about it. If it makes you feel better to [go back and check], go back then." Although it was painful for me at the time, it helped lead to my ultimate recovery. As a follow-up to this thought and having the benefit of hindsight, it would have been helpful prior to my diagnosis and early on in my therapy for her be armed with the questions I have listed under the Checkpoints.

Remember if you become a crutch and tell your loved one how to deal with OCD or more specifically what decisions to make, it will be difficult for the person you care about to get better. Remind your loved one that he or she doesn't have to be perfect. Give your loved one a lot of encouragement and hugs. Remind your loved one that he or she is one of God's children, he or she is special, he or she has value, and he or she is loved.

And for you—your job is difficult too. Don't be afraid to tap into your own network of support. It always helps to talk to someone else, particularly someone who knows what you are experiencing. Good luck to you. And one more thing: you don't have to be perfect either.

S hannon Shy is a civilian attorney with the Department of the Navy. He and his wife Debbie have three children—Alex, Andrew, and Samantha—and live in Dale City, Virginia, just south of Washington DC.

After graduating from Southwest Missouri State University and the University of Missouri-Columbia School of Law, he went on active duty with the Marine Corps. In 1999, after eleven years of active duty, Shannon accepted a civil service position in Washington D.C. with the Department of the Navy Office of General Counsel and a Marine Corps Reserve commission. In 2007, he retired from the Marine Corps Reserve as a Lieutenant Colonel.

In a volunteer capacity, Shannon has coached youth football, baseball, and soccer. In 2003, he co-founded the Northern Virginia Youth Athletic Association (NVYAA), a non-profit youth football and cheerleading organization dedicated to excellence in athletics, scholastics, and community service. Serving over two hundred children between ages 5 and 15, NVYAA teams won four American Youth Football (AYF) national championships from 2005 to 2007. From 2007 to 2009, Shannon served as AYF's National Membership Director. A "ham" behind the mike, Shannon volunteers as stadium announcer for C.D. Hylton High School's football program and for the AYF national championships and national all-star game.